JULES' GARDENING

JULES' GARDENING

Julian Vaudrey

ATHENA PRESS
LONDON

First Published 2006 by
ATHENA PRESS
Queen's House, 2 Holly Road
Twickenham TW1 4EG
United Kingdom

Printed for Athena Press

Preface

Mental illness – what is it?

Depression, psychosis, anxiety attacks, schizophrenia, nervous breakdowns, manic depression, phobias and paranoia.

Who is afflicted?

A large percentage of Western society is afflicted at some point in their lives with mental illness. Much research is still continuing; new remedies and medicines are being devised. Much mental illness is drug-related, but this is not the case with myself. I am a heavy smoker, but that is my only vice. I have never touched drugs.

I don't believe I have had or suffered one of these illnesses, but I have displayed symptoms of each. In a vulnerable state of mind, I caught, bit by bit, the illness of others. However, I have never been a depressive; a psychiatrist told me that very early on in November 2000.

Four sessions with a well-acknowledged psychiatrist led to no diagnosis, except for an acknowledgement of my fear of women. My mother was forever begging for a diagnosis, desperate to be informed I had a mental illness. Into each session, I took with me a copy of the Bible. Religion has helped me through these troubled times.

In the CHL (Centre Hospitalier Luxembourg) they diagnosed me with psychosis. This turned out to be the biggest misdiagnosis ever. Psychosis my arse!

My illness has been mysterious. It is God-given and only God will cure it.

He has. Praise Him!

Chapter One

I've done it! I've made it! I am home and dry – Hallelujah! It has been a long haul, lasting just over four years, almost to the day! In and out, round about, up and down. Now I am free, free as a bird. It feels good, so good. The crap I've been through, I never expected it; it came upon me. It was my fate. Never again!

At school I had my whole future ahead of me. At university I always had my studies to look forward to. Year after year there was always a goal. Then I had ideas for after university, ideas of being a manager on my father's estate. Vague ideas, nothing concrete. Ideas of returning to Moscow and perhaps living there. Ideas of going to Uganda. Ideas of doing a postgraduate degree, becoming a priest. Then, bang! Before I knew it, I was inside a psychiatric ward, locked up and examined. Put on the spot. What went wrong? Why was I there? What could I do?

I was subjected to medicine when I always had a firm belief that I didn't require medication of any sort. I was against all pills, even for a headache.

Do I take it? What's it for? Why do I need it? What have I done to deserve it? God, why have you forsaken me?

What went wrong? In short, everything. My relationship with Marta ended. My love, my life. All my dreams were dashed. At first, I couldn't accept it. For three months I couldn't accept it. I kept going back. We were in the same town, Durham, so I saw her all the time but I couldn't have her. God kept us apart.

Having been to Tenerife together for a week pre-Christmas, our friendship escalated into a love affair. We talked about marriage. I proposed and asked her father for her hand in marriage. Marta and her mother were constantly asking me what I envisaged for our future together. I went blank every time they questioned me. It annoyed and frustrated me because I simply wanted her to trust that everything would be fine. But that wasn't enough.

Back in Durham, it was tough. We were so close, yet I couldn't touch her. Once, I thought the damage was repaired. We were lying together in her room in college. I thought I had her, then there was a knock on the door – another student called to tell us that Marta's mum was on the phone. I had to leave. Friends, thereafter, discouraged me from seeing her. Lee Ray was one. I would get hurt even more, he said.

Marta had invited me to Tenerife. Friendship turned to sexual relations. I didn't want it to happen. I believed in no sex before marriage. She very obviously wanted it. One night, instead of our praying together, she invited me to get into bed with her. Reluctantly, I did, and I felt my link with God break. I came straight away. I hadn't made love for more than two and a half years. I got off the bed and prayed, 'God have mercy on me. Lord have mercy on me.'

I've just started writing this book and I am so excited. Scooter (my favourite music group, and every German teenager's idol) is playing on the TV. I have had a good day. I am alone in my flat in a quiet place called Altrier, which is on the outskirts of Luxembourg. My friend Billy has just called and he is going off on holiday with his girlfriend, Romana, to a place called Villefranche in the South of France. I have just returned from holiday myself. My girlfriend and I went to Istanbul where her mother lives. We stayed in a hotel in the centre of town and did plenty of exciting things. We went with her son, Kimmy. He is amazing. Wherever we went, he brought joy, and other people received him warmly.

Back to Luxembourg. I work as a gardener. This morning I worked with my Yugoslav colleague, Edin. We shovelled twenty-seven barrows of horse dung from the front of a house to the garden. It took one hour and ten minutes. For this we received a feeble pay of €100. We could have asked for more, but I lost confidence. The family was a nice family and I have a problem with charging people I like.

I am a friendly guy. I was born in Belgium, but I have lived most of my life in Luxembourg. I have a good and loving family. I have friends all around the world. I speak seven languages and I have travelled widely. Sometimes I dabble on the piano. I have a belief in a Christian God and He helps me. I have just prayed that He will help me write this book. I am certain He will.

I love the work I do. I love it, tough as it is. I was thinking this just two days ago: it's the best job I could have. Every day is different, ever a challenge. I get job satisfaction and variety. The only problem is that it doesn't really challenge the intellect.

Anyway, yesterday afternoon I joined up with my friends, Jim, Lionel and Pete, from the rehabilitation hospital, where I was a patient about eight months ago. Lionel was much better. He has started working and is feeling good; he has come out of himself. Jim, sadly, was not so good. His eyes were enormous – wide and staring, and he was very subdued. Pete, as usual, was on good form. All three are good friends of mine.

After going swimming, we went for a drink together in Auchan, the shopping mall on the Kirchberg. We discussed things like life after death and whether we were scared of death or not. We concluded that we will all be judged, and that prospect is a fairly scary affair. My dear mother, with whom I have had many problems and who is presently walking in Ecuador, believes that there will be different levels in heaven: the saints at the very top end, and the not so good a bit further down. I believe, as the Bible states, that there is both a heaven and a hell, and that hell is the separation from God; if, throughout your life, you tell God to bugger off, then, finally, at the end of your life, he will say, 'Fine, off you go; you didn't want me. Now go to hell.' Not funny, really. I think it is safer for all to believe, just in case hell does exist.

I have just mentioned my mother. She is called Ann-Maria and is great. She has a faith, too, and is very good-hearted, very proud and very forgiving. She decided to do another of her trips and finds herself this time in Ecuador, where she is with a group climbing Cotopaxi, I think. Just yesterday she reached the summit. She doesn't sit around twiddling her thumbs. She is very energetic and adventurous. She has suffered much with sore shoulders, back problems and neck aches, but she battles on. The rest of the year when she isn't walking, she fulfils her role as wife and housewife. Soon she will have grandchildren.

I say soon, because I am highly sexed and I have a girlfriend whom I want to marry and with whom I want children – lots of them. My sister, Susannah, is pregnant and has been so for three months. She is married to a gentleman called Godfrey, a northerner from Preston. They met in Durham and married in August 2001. Theirs was the first wedding I ever went to. I always told myself that the first wedding I would go to would be my own. I had dreams of marrying Marta on Holy Island, near the Scottish border: just a priest, ourselves and maybe a couple of friends. I wanted to take her to Ireland for our honeymoon.

Susannah and Godfrey's wedding was a phenomenal affair. It happened in Uselberg, where my parents live and they tied the knot in the local church and then had the reception in our large house, which has a massive garden. There was a marquee in the garden and a red carpet leading down to it, flanked with large candles. I was with my girlfriend, Simmy, who became very jealous because I danced with all the girls, most memorably with Godfrey's sister, Lara.

After Susannah, I have two brothers, Rich and Ken. Rich is one year younger than me and he is working in Luxembourg for part of the EIB group – the European Investment Fund. He takes pride in driving fancy cars. At the moment he drives a Mercedes SLK 350.

Ken is in Russia in St Petersburg where he is studying for an MBA. He has a delightful girlfriend called Mika. She is four years younger than him. In a recent email he complained of an alcoholic whose stench found its way into his flat! Poor him.

Anyway, back to me. It's morning now and I had a good sleep. I'm not sure I dreamt of anything last night. But the weather is perfect – blue skies, frost, and the sun is just rising. An ideal winter's day. I am a winter man. I have always liked winter – no leaves on the trees, and dry most of the time. A low sun during the day and frost or snow on the ground. The arrival of spring imminent, or something to look forward to.

I am wearing Simmy's scarf, the one she gave me for my birthday. Oh yeah, let me tell you about that! It was my birthday on 29 December. I was twenty-eight. (During my twenty-seventh birthday I had a sort of feeling that I would like to end my life that year, like Jim Morrison and others. That is by the by. I always had reason to live.) I got up at my girlfriend's and had a breakfast of eggs and bacon. Then I drove to my flat, picked up some stuff and met my landlord – a nice chap called Gary with whom I always spoke in Luxembourgish, a language I have picked up over the past few years. It is a dialect of German mixed with French. Most people don't appreciate it. But I do. I think it's fantastic. So much fun to speak. A bit like Dutch. You can say things so directly in Luxembourgish.

I then drove down the Moselle, the river that divides Luxembourg from Germany. I stopped on the way for a beer, telling everyone that it was my birthday and then proceeded a bit further to a place called Remich, where I met a chap called Don Giver in front of the bandstand. I loved this guy. He is the son of Rachel, a woman who has given me 'prayerful support', as she calls it, over the recent past. She has deep faith and she writes down everyone she wants to pray for. She challenged me about that, but I simply remember everyone without having to write down their names. In quiet moments, I pray for my friends and family and extended family, asking God to bless them and meet their needs.

Rachel's husband is called Peter, like my father, and his son is called Robert, who is a cool kid and does ballet. He has had a whole string of girlfriends and presently has an extremely beautiful one from Australia, whose name I can't remember. I met her at my friend's birthday party the day after my own.

Anyway, Don and I met in front of the bandstand, walked around for a bit (we didn't really know each other), and then chose a Chinese restaurant that I wanted to go to. He told me that the two most important women in his life, his mother and his girlfriend, Louisa, both have spoken very highly of me. I was flattered. He told me how he was car-jacked in London, which prompted him to move. He went to the Cayman Islands where he practiced law before moving back to Luxembourg. I am glad he is here.

We talked about Louisa a little, who is still suffering from depression. She needs a miracle and a lot of prayer.

After lunch, while walking, we briefly touched on the subject of homosexuality and the church's regard to it and the literacy of the Bible. He told me some truths about the chaplain, who, amongst various, disapproved of homosexuality. Amongst other things, Don is very pro-gay, but is not gay himself. I have no problem with gay people. They are generally very nice people. Using the word 'nice' prompts me to think of my English teacher at the European School, Mr Fisher, who told us never to use the word 'nice' in creative writing. I don't care – sometimes I find it the perfect word. Says just what you want it to say.

On the subject or question of suicide, I never knew whether in this life it was permissible. I debated the issue for so long. I couldn't move forward in my life because I refused to let go of trying to kill myself. I wanted to know how religion deals with suicide, but no one would tell me. I have no fear of death, so I thought it would be OK. God would forgive me. I now know life is not one's own. My life doesn't belong to me. My life is not my own to take. God gave us life, so God will take it when the time comes. My psychiatrist told me that you can't do it; you have your life to live; you have your life's mission to fulfil. I now understand that he's right. But I now believe I went through that phase for a reason. The reason, I believe, was so I could separate myself from the grasp of my mother.

Some action needed to be taken. I was revolving in circles at home: being injected with Haldol (Haldoperidol) on a monthly basis, unable to make progress under my own steam, and few others lending a helping hand. I know it sounds strange. Those nearest and dearest to me took me for granted and now they appreciate me more, which is exactly what I wanted, I think.

It's all uphill now. I know it is. By the day, life is getting better and better and easier and easier.

Today I've been painting, which was great fun. We went to buy the paint and were given a cap, each with 'Robin' written on the side – a family name. The day went quickly. There were no mistakes, except the colour may be too dark. We had a couple of fag breaks and coffee. I don't advocate smoking, but it goes with this sort of work.

Chapter Two

Hallelujah, Jesus! Praise be to God! Life goes on, as does Jules' diary. What would you like to hear today? Tomorrow is Tuesday and the next day Wednesday. Tomorrow we have a Luxembourgish lesson, then some more painting and I may even try my hand on the rugby field. I used to play a lot of rugby – I started at the age of eight. It is a passion of mine, a wonderful game, full of skill and talent. They say that soccer is a game for gentlemen played by thugs, and rugby is a game for thugs played by gentlemen. Believe what you wish. Both games have their perks. Both can be very exciting to watch.

Rugby: I started playing at eight years old in the European School in Luxembourg. We had three coaches, Mr Wikins, Mr David and Mr Bertram, a Belgian. (Talking of Belgians, yesterday morning I went for a walk in the woods with one before going to church.) At that young age we only played eight-a-side – three up front and five back. I loved it then. So much fun. I was always a fierce tackler. We had such a good team. We won all the tournaments and generally played in the French league – Alsace-Lorraine – and every Saturday we would travel somewhere different. Some of the friends I used to play with were Keith James, Noel Bray, Bill Andrews, Alex Wikins and Dick Sage. We used to pull moonies out the back window of the bus. We went to places like Longwy, Verdun, Metz, Nancy and Thionville. The youngest age category was known as Poussins, then Benjamins, then Minims.

I was very good and always fancied that I would be a great player later in life. Dick Sage recently assured me that he could always rely on me – I didn't miss a tackle.

At the age of thirteen I was sent, voluntarily, to Rugby School, the birthplace of the game. In my first year there we did a re-enactment of the first game ever played. I remember that I tackled William Webb Ellis when I was meant to let him run through. It was a massive event; we all wore period costumes. I remember my father meeting an ex-girlfriend of his in the crowd. I was at Rugby

School for five years – thirteen to eighteen. The game was played very differently there. Straight into fifteen-a-side, I really disliked it at first. My team-mates were very arrogant and all came from good prep schools. Instead of encouraging each other, they would undermine you. They forever accused me of dropping the ball. I was doing my best – they couldn't tackle like me. That's why I always made the first team. My best rugby years were at the European School, by far. It was much more fun. Freer. I never really understood fifteen-a-side, although I always made the A-team.

Tomorrow I will try playing rugby again. I may have a few problems because of my accident. In March 2003, I deliberately drove my car into a tree at 120 kmph. I didn't die, otherwise I wouldn't be writing this. I broke both ankles, my femur and my neck, displacing a couple of teeth also. They had to cut me out of the car. It was a foolish act. I now understand that I did it for attention; I didn't really want to die. The recovery was slow, and was hindered by my psychological problems. But I recovered, and now I am fit and fighting again, working and socialising and going to church, amongst other things.

Right now, life couldn't really be better. I don't believe it when people say that the best years of your life are at university. Life doesn't have to go downhill – nonsense – it should improve with age. It says in the Bible '...enter the Kingdom of God as children.' I know many old people who are young in spirit, which I believe is the way to be. The key is to stay active and busy and do things for other people, not simply focusing on yourself and your ageing process. I had that sensation whilst in hospital; I hated the feeling that I was watching myself grow older. You need to exist and be involved in whatever that may be. In society there are so many opportunities to be involved, for example, joining a club or society. The simple act of meeting people from other walks of life. I learnt about that whilst hitch-hiking. I hitch-hiked thousands of miles in my university years. And it's not over yet. I love it. I have a whole philosophy for hitch-hiking. Just being beside the road and putting your fate in others' hands. If you hitch, I think, you believe in God. You are saying, 'There is nothing I can do; I am relying on chance.' You live in hope and you do as much as you can: smile stupidly, dance, prance about, gesticulate. It is pure chance if someone stops, and when they do, you are ecstatic; you are so grateful. Amen.

I need to mention here that yesterday, after church, I told a man called Joseph Dirkins, a father of four, that I had just come back from Istanbul. He told me that he had once tried to hitch there from London, but had no luck leaving Greece, so had stayed there. It's a gamble – you either have the patience for it, or you don't.

I asked my brother's girlfriend, Letiza, after lunch yesterday what the best piece of news she had ever been given was. She answered, after a considerable pause, that probably it was hearing that her father didn't have cancer. Nice one. My father wasn't sure, but then agreed with Rich that it was probably getting his job at the European Investment Bank; my brother likewise – getting his job with the European Investment Fund. Mine was getting my A level results. I had worked really hard for them and got three A grades. I had the time to work because I hadn't been given the role of head of house, even though I was a strong candidate. My house was called Schoolfield. From the beginning, people told me that I would be given the position, but I was caught drinking in my penultimate year and, as I always say, the housemaster couldn't twist me around his little finger, like he would with the other candidate. I had so many ideas for when I was head of house – I would have changed so much.

I did French, German and Maths for my A levels. The first two were really easy, since I came from Luxembourg. I struggled with the literature, but we read some interesting stuff. In Maths I had already got an A by January (it was modular). So, for two terms I could concentrate solely on French and German. Every evening I went to the language laboratory to listen to, or watch, foreign TV. I also did lots of sport: tennis, squash and jogging, and I was captain of judo.

The head of school was a chap called Bert Johnson; he was a real superstar. In the school performance of *The Pirates of Penzance* he was the Pirate King. He was very popular – a very self-confident and talented boy. In the first year, both he and I were picked as ideal pupils (pupils who led an all-round lifestyle – a balance between intellect, musical ability and sport). As a thirteen-year-old, I was very keen. I had been a Boy Scout in Luxembourg and had been made a sixer and patrol leader. At

Rugby I joined the RAF Cadet Force and I was made a sergeant. We had a lot of fun in the early days in the RAF. We would make fun of the other sergeant – a guy called Richard Wittage – who took it very seriously. He was very power happy. I was accused of this trait too, when, at the age of fourteen, the four of us at the end of the dormitory were given the responsibility of keeping the rest of the room quiet. I was teased because of this.

There were two dormitories in Schoolfield, one of thirty-two, one of twenty-eight. They were a lot of fun, but later I found them a bore. My peers were very inconsiderate – they would squabble until the small hours. Now these dormitories are no more. Both have been converted into bedsits. I would love to go back there and see the changes. Schoolfield was right on the Close, the central school grounds. To get to chapel we simply had to walk across the rugger pitch. Usually, only the prefects could do so; the rest had to walk around. Because I was captain of judo, I could cross the pitch.

A few of us in the house were always late for chapel, which started at eight thirty in the morning every Tuesday, Thursday and Friday. Chapel on Sundays was optional; the alternative was forum, to which they invited outside speakers.

Enough about Rugby School – I can expand later. What I wish to say now is that every day for me is like the weekend – there is no difference. Work for me isn't work in the common understanding of the word. I enjoy working, manual labour. It frees the soul. Talking of souls, Russia has a soul, or at least they say it has. If you go there, like I did in 1998/9, you realise there is some sort of attractive power. You either love it or hate it. You have to be tough to go to Russia. It is a very brutal place. But you go beyond the surface and you realise the warmth of people's hearts. The Russians have to sport a brave face; life there is a fight. If you don't push to get on a tram, you never will; you have to play along. There is a very good book by Hedrick Smith about the Russians called, funnily enough, *The Russians.*

Russia is a brutal place. If you are not strong enough you get eaten up, swallowed alive. In Russia, people will do anything to survive – pick up empty bottles, sell anything from needles to shampoo to ice cream. The average age of a Russian man is only about sixty. The Russians talk critically of the Americans, yet they are equally materialistic themselves, if given the chance. They have an unfounded illusion of the United States and they believe that life is a bed of roses there. Many emigrate and then find that they miss their own people. There is a phenomenon known as the brain drain: all the best minds leave Russia in search of a better life elsewhere – London, Paris, New York. It is such a shame that they leave at a time when their country needs them most. Russia is very corrupt.

I have to add that the human resources in Russia are phenomenal. There is hope for the country, even if it is so fundamentally screwed up. Russians have suffered such a tragic past: 20 million Russians died in the war, millions more in the Revolution and an equal amount in Stalin's purges. If the government can deal with the corruption, then there is hope. The Russian people deserve a better life. The country, I believe, is blessed. There is hope – there must be hope, although the country is deeply warped. I sensed that in my short stay there. In the hostel, we foreigners, about twenty of us in all, frequently discussed the fate of the Russians, and in the classroom (I taught English there) we had some very positive discussions. We concluded that Russia isn't ready for a democracy yet. But there is hope. There must be hope!

Chapter Three

It's about ten o'clock and I have just spoken to my father on the phone. I rang him. He hasn't eaten yet, but he told me that he has recently acquired a Caprese machine, a machine that slices Mozzarella cheese and tomatoes. Caprese must be one of the most delicious starters.

Our family has been to Italy a lot, which is probably why I enjoy Italian food so much. When I was young we went every summer for fifteen years. We went to a place called Punta Ala, between Grossetto and Pisa. The place was a campsite situated in some woods, with squirrels and lizards running all over it. There was a real sense of community there and it was easy to make friends. Each family had their own allotment, surrounded by trees. We would buy produce from the local supermarket or from the market in town and prepare our meals on camping stoves. If you walked down one of the lanes, the smell of grilled fish or pasta would fill the air. After lunch the campsite would be totally quiet, with everyone taking a siesta.

My father, Ken and I windsurfed a lot, braving the ocean. Sometimes we would eat dinner together on the beach. It was always a real family occasion and we would see the same friends year after year. Generally, there was a mix of Italians and Germans, all relatively wealthy. There was time to seriously relax. There was a lot of lazing about, doing nothing, reading or sitting on the beach. It was a time to gently ponder the oncoming academic year. Godfrey, Susannah's husband, has been there a few times, as has Simmy, Kit, Ken's friend, Bridget, Rich's girlfriend and my good friend Nicholas Swithe, who loved it there.

I have just been on the phone to Nick Holt. He always makes me laugh. Presently, he is working on a film about obese people. He works freelance, filming documentaries. He was a housemate of mine at Durham and is a very clever young man, very powerful and very manipulative. He knows he is very funny and people underestimate him. Underneath all the bravado he is very honest and good. At Durham, I felt that I was the only one who really knew him. He doesn't take himself very seriously, always joking and making fun. He knows me very well too and knows how to make me laugh. He went to Uppingham and had a circle of friends who were all very close, all lads – the ultimate lads. They had their own language: 'Get out', 'whookie', '*donnez-le-hatch*', to say 'the big *au-revoir*', 'pugwhoopter' and '*no fash mal*', the Portuguese expression meaning, 'not a problem'.

He gave me a lot of problems in my first year. He was great when I was alone with him, but when surrounded by others, he'd put on an act and either ignore me or put me down. He had his image at stake. I didn't like it, but I stuck by him and I trust that today he is cool.

I discovered Christianity whilst at university. Hallelujah! I came full circle, as I had been brought up to believe. We used to go to church on Sundays. We participated in Sunday school at junior church, where we did God-related activities under the guidance of the leaders, Bob and Felicity. I was in the choir there for a year or two; my sister, Susannah, and I used to go to our friends' house after school, before choir practice (this is the same family at whose house Edin and I shovelled the horse dung on Saturday). They are an incredible family; all have either been to Oxford or Cambridge. Peter and Emma have four children – three girls and one boy – and they are all very musical. Peter is the choir master; Susan, the second daughter, has married a Spaniard. I wanted to employ her in my painting business. She accepted, but is moving to London soon.

Christianity – I came full circle. I was unhappy during my first year at Durham. I was obviously searching for something. I got drunk every night and avidly read the newspapers and books. I was being manipulated by Nicholas and had no real friends. I was supposedly still in a relationship with Bianca, my Slovak girlfriend, but I didn't want to be tied down and I let her know that. She was my first love. We met in Slovakia in September 1996. She was beautiful and I instantly fell for her, but at that time she didn't have much of a life; she was always studying. She was very nice, very pure. I never made love to her.

Amazing! I have made a remarkable recovery. It's incredible! From doing absolutely nothing about seven months ago, to having a life now. I am living on my own, going to courses, Luxo yesterday and Russian today, earning my bread, going to church. Long live life! It tastes so sweet. I had better knock on some wood, because you never know. My Luxembourgish isn't as good as I thought it was; there is plenty of room for improvement.

19 January 2005

Right, I am off swimming. It is a Wednesday and it has snowed again. This morning I popped in on an old client – not that she's old, but she was one of my first clients. I sat down in her kitchen and started reading the *Herald Tribune* whilst she was unpacking her shopping and cooking mussels. I started talking about, or describing, the weather in detail and she told me I should be a weatherman. I know I am not quite better yet, because I am still taking my medicine.

I have just spoken to three people on the dog and bone – cockney rhyming slang for telephone – my granny, my sister and Uta, my girlfriend. My grandmother, Shevon, sounded fine, and is about to have an operation on her knee on 8 February, poor her. I joked that she only had two knees. She expected me to be my cousin, Kristina, who is getting married this summer to a chap called Pete, a South African. I have only met him once, briefly, so cannot comment. I trust that she has picked someone relatively cool and high-spirited. They have been living together for some time already, as Susannah, my sister, did with her husband (for two or three years, I think).

Not me! I wish to do things differently. Like my mother, I don't believe in living together before you are married. What's the point? To find out if you can live together or like each other? You have a whole lifetime to discover that. I think the old-fashioned way. You should already know you love each other, then you get married, then you live together. Marriage, I believe, is all about commitment. You will see things through, whatever the cost, life-long. Marriage isn't a joke; I believe it is a promise before God and that is serious – you promise that you will love each other for life, through thick and thin. You can't just walk out. Divorce is a lengthy and costly process; there's always a lot of money and heartache involved. Weddings have become such a performance – people organise gigantic affairs at a tremendous cost. The pressure put on the bride and groom is enormous. Marriages for the super-rich and famous that are conducted entirely under the media spotlight – for example, Claudia Schiffer, David Beckham and Posh Spice, Tom Cruise and Katie Holmes. So much pressure to perform.

Then I spoke to Susannah, who is about three months pregnant. The expression in Yugoslav is '*trudna žena*', which means 'difficult woman'. She now knows the baby's size: 15 cm long. She sounded concerned about my grandmother, who she says is struggling a lot. I wanted to tell Granny that she must be fighting fit for my wedding in the summer or next year; perhaps that will give her some motivation. Then I spoke to Uta, who keeps telling me that she loves me, which is nice. She didn't drink today, she told me. Great!

Chapter Four

Back to the aforementioned birthday on 29 December. After lunch with Don Giver I drove into town and met up with my friend Jim Perrin who works for Deutsche Bank, here in Luxembourg. We were sort of school friends and have kept in constant touch ever since. He has been a very faithful friend and is a very soft-spoken, composed sort of guy. He is married and has two children. Bella is very sweet and extremely charming, and Cynth is a clever girl. Jim lent me his whizzer (lawnmower), which didn't work very well, so I was forced to give it back. Machines and I don't really go very well together, but that is another story. I am very much anti-democracy, machines and technology.

In the evening we celebrated in style. We had booked a table for twelve and ended up having about seventeen. Kimmy behaved very well, and when the cake was brought to the table I was summoned to make a speech. I enjoy these occasions and always rise to the challenge. I stood up and someone pointed to the music stand on which there was a microphone. I proceeded to greet the entire restaurant. I told my friends that I loved them and that I was sure that our paths would cross many times in 2005. Then I sat down. End of story.

My life is getting better and better, forever on the up. I feel more stable and I am sort of enjoying a routine now. Today, I didn't work but I kept myself occupied. After swimming at the giant Olympic pool, where I did twenty-five lengths, I went to a shopping centre called Auchan and bought myself some bananas, and some Hugo Boss boxer shorts – at a price: €38 (10 per cent discount). I have been wearing my last pair for two weeks now and they have marks in them, so it was high time to buy another pair.

After shopping, I went to the Pushkin Institute where I have my weekly Russian lesson. I arrived early and had the privilege of meeting a sculptor who had his work on show. He had been brought over from Russia – the Urals, to be exact – for a whole month! He offered me coffee and we enjoyed a cigarette together outside. Then I chanced upon a dance school, which, a little later, Uta and I may attend.

After the Russian lesson I hit the motorway for Ettlebruck, where I had an appointment with my psychiatrist. I had a bone to pick with him, but he said he was only trying to do his job, which is fair enough. We exchanged seats. I sat in his revolving chair and he on the single stool. I was showing him who was boss! I only have one more appointment with him and that is it. I want to slowly come off my medication.

I am sitting in my flat in my dirty boxer shorts, having just had a shower and I am wondering what to write next. I want to write all about a very special experience I had in my year off between school and university, in the Republic of Slovakia. I will then revert to the rest of my day, which has a very interesting conclusion. So here goes.

Slovakia, Slovakia, Slovakia: the country in which I left my heart; a very blessed country. So unknown and so little heard of. The capital is Bratislava, and it lies in the heart of Europe. It borders Ukraine to the east and Poland to the north (with which it shares the High Tatra Mountains), Hungary to the south and Australia to the west – only joking – Austria to the west. Vienna is only about half an hour's drive from Bratislava. Budapest, the capital of Hungary is just over the border to the south. It also shares a border with the Czech Republic, its good friend to the north-west. It was, as you should know, formerly part of Czechoslovakia before the Velvet Revolution. My good pal, John Bisham, and I travelled throughout all these countries on numerous occasions. Our first weekend trip was to a mountain called Chopok, where John very bravely attempted to ski for the first time. I am an experienced skier and was only too glad to aid a forlorn first-timer. He was always a very unlucky chap, but he could always giggle at himself. I believe, now, fortune has changed for him, since he has landed himself with a good job and is engaged to be married. I hope I will be invited to his wedding. I should be. We went on some excellent trips together – we had a slightly manic experience in Prague, where we tried to overturn a Trabant!

At Easter time, 1996, John and I, in search of some Austrian girls we had met in Vienna on a previous trip, hitch-hiked through six countries in just four days. We had a total of about forty lifts. We hitched through Hungary, Austria, Italy (Trieste), Slovenia and Croatia.

Slovakia is a beautiful country, situated in the middle of Europe; breathtaking scenery, magnificent castles, pretty towns and villages, a warm-hearted people, very Catholic. Much of the land is inhabited by gypsies, a very poor folk – Romanies, they call them. They are very musical, I believe. The Slovaks condemn them; they blame them for crime. Supposedly they steal crops, especially potatoes, from the fields. They live in small huts with corrugated iron roofs. Ian and I once chanced upon one of these small communities. Naked children were playing in a stream; others came to pester us. In retrospect, we were very lucky. Our lives could have been at stake as we were told that not long before, a foreigner had been killed in one of those villages. The Slovaks are very nationalistic. To coin the phrase, *Na Slovensko, po Slovenský*, meaning, in Slovakia, speak Slovak.

I greatly enjoyed my sojourn in Slovakia, from beginning to end, taking in nature and the scenes. There is an area to the east just before the town of Koshitze, called Slovenský Rai (Slovak Paradise) – forests on rolling hills with very interesting walks or hikes; wooden ladders, caves and metal ladders make the way more exciting. There were some superb views. It was a real adventure hiking there. You stay in small, self-catering huts on the edge of the forest in a clearing. Betty, Cassie, John and I had such a good time there; we laughed so much. We ate simply and celebrated Betty's birthday. Ian had managed to find her a copy of the *Keighley News*, the local paper where she is from. Betty, John and I taught English there (more like helping in the classroom), and Cassie taught art. We were close and enjoyed each other's company. Cassie and Betty were still doing PGCEs in England and they were in Slovakia for teaching practice. Ian and I were sent to this amazing country by the organisation GAP, based in Reading. Our agent was a man called Mr Smith, a pensioner. I would recommend anyone to apply through GAP to do a placement in Slovakia. The beer is cheap and the girls are really something – real head-turners. I remember turning up at a gym and watching all the girls do their aerobics; I had never seen anything like it. Like that film with Jim Carey, my eyes nearly left their sockets!

I lost my innocence in Slovakia to Cassie and then had a couple of casual Slovak girlfriends, one called Wanda and the other Luba. The end came upon us quickly. We had made so many friends; it was very sad to have to leave. Returning to the West was tough. We had had a very fulfilling and exciting six months. Both Ian and I had university and careers to look forward to; we were both out of public school, where we had been restricted, to say the least. In Slovakia we had cheap beer at hand, and women. After teaching in the spring and summer months, we would all sit together in the beer gardens, downing pint after pint until we hobbled home to our respective domains or flats.

I had earned good money in Luxembourg beforehand, working as a data-inputter for Flemings Fund Management for five months, earning a decent grand a month, so in the east, in Slovakia, I was a relatively rich chap. For my teaching I earned about eighty quid a month, enough to buy Crunchy Nut cereal from Tesco's, at least twice a week.

The week before I left, Rich came out to visit me and we all went rafting down the Pieniny River. We took a crate of beer with us and laughed all the way – John entertained us all.

Furthermore, I was a hit in the classroom. The kids adored me – God knows why! I was young and fresh and relatively innocent compared with their usual grumpy, bespectacled mistresses. All I did was play games with them, and I took to teaching like a fish to water. I never prepared my lessons the day before, always last minute. The sensation of walking down the corridor before the lessons, not knowing what to expect, was exhilarating. One of my colleagues, Alex, was very envious of my job, since he had to be a little more serious and teach grammar sometimes. He included me in the school magazine. Another teacher, Guy, promised to take me flying in a glider.

Having written this makes me want to tell you all about the other trips I have been so lucky to have made: Thailand, Australia, Jordan, Morocco, South Africa, Canada, Singapore and Bosnia and just recently Portugal and Istanbul. If I do I will just bore you. I went to Thailand on my own in June 1996; Australia, on the rugby tour in 1994; Jordan, to see my younger brother Ken; Morocco to visit Rich; South Africa, courtesy of my good school friend, Dan Woolsey, whose father worked in Johannesburg for a cigarette company. I went instead of Dan's brother. Incidentally, in Canada on a skiing trip with the lads from Durham, I became famous by doing a streak at an ice-hockey game. I made history one cold

Friday evening. Calgary Flames were playing against Florida and for some reason or another I decided to take off all my clothes and run on to the rink, only sporting a whistle – it makes a good story.

Tomorrow I will continue, but now it's time for bed. We are painting again tomorrow and must be on good form with no mistakes if we want more business.

10.30 a.m., Friday, 21 January

Yesterday, on the way to work, I stopped off at a brasserie in a place called Larochette and ordered a coffee and some chips. Then Victoria walked in.

Work was fun. Edin and I painted the hall at home. We started at midday and were finished by seven o'clock for a fee of €400, which we shared. I have a philosophy about work that you can build up such a rhythm whilst working that you get completely absorbed in what you are doing. Read Tolstoy's *Anna Karenina*, in which there is a very vivid passage about the peasants labouring, sweat pouring from their brows – that's us at work.

Sorry, yesterday I didn't have much to write about. Today I do. Let's go! Hallelujah, Jesus! Stupid President Bush of the United States of America gave his inauguration speech today and, apparently, he used the word 'freedom' twenty-nine times according to the British press, and forty-one times according to the French. Now what do we have to say about that? Don't listen to Bush, please. He is a rogue. What is freedom? Are the American people free when they all live in big houses in compounds, with tight security and big cars, because they are afraid that they will be burgled? Is that free? Is the man himself, Bush, George Bush, free when he has to travel abroad with a whole army of bodyguards and entourage, afraid that he will be assassinated? Is that free? Is that really free? Are the American people really free when members of their population are in jail for offences such as murder and rape? Are they all afraid that they will commit those offences again? Isn't it society that has produced those sorts of people? My God, what has happened in the United States? What a fucked up country, excuse my French. Bombing the rest of the world because they are afraid of being attacked, trying to impose a democracy on the rest of the world as if they know best. High fences, guard dogs and compounds? I don't know. However, I should limit my judgement as I have never been to the States – the closest I have been is Canada, where I did my streak.

You know what freedom is? I can tell you because I have experienced it and I am experiencing it now. True/real freedom is not owning anything and living cheap. Hard to achieve, yes, that I am realising. At the moment I have a flat and a car. I did have a girlfriend, but I have just dumped her. In the West we build up so much into our lives, hence we add complications.

I have just spoken to Uta and she expressed doubt about our relationship, saying that I was a bit distant towards her. I had the opportunity to tell her that I was feeling a tad depressed and she said 'me also'. I don't know why I feel depressed. I have just woken up like that. Maybe I slept too long, maybe drinking and staying out late on Friday night didn't help.

It's frosty outside again and the sky is blue and now I have to go to church, I want to. I enjoy church. I love being with a community of people, all with the same purpose. A lot has happened this week, but I haven't really been very faithful to you, my dear readers. I love what I am doing, writing this book. So I need to find a healthy compromise between living in the day and scribbling. Off to church – back soon. God bless.

What's up? Gave my life to Jesus again last night. I meditated and I invited Jesus into my life. I haven't done that for a long time. It is a serious step. I asked God for forgiveness and made a vow that I would amend my ways. I have taken a serious step. Jesus, you are my Lord and my Saviour, and I will do everything in my power to follow you.

That's all very well, but then we went to Brussels yesterday to fetch my Yugoslav colleague, Edin's, passport. I sort of justified the trip by saying it was for recruitment purposes, since we met Edin's friend, Marko, who isn't working, but is a solid lad and I would love to have him on my team. It took a while to find the embassy, but after we did, things went like clockwork. Marko was waiting for us in the embassy, and then he kindly invited us back to his big flat, fairly close to the centre. We had my girlfriend's car, an Opel something, which was fun to drive around in. Marko served us hamburgers with a choice of either Turkish or Moroccan bread and the typical Yugoslav cheese and pickled peppers. This other chap randomly turned up, an uncle or something, with piercing eyes and a large forehead. He gave us a spiel about Milosevic and his regime and the student demonstrations that took place in Serbia back in 1996/97. He said the worst war was the media war because the people didn't have a clue what was going on then. They were being fed bollocks on their own TV channels. If you remember there were hundreds of thousands of people on the streets before the Americans started to bomb Serbia.

Let me tell you about a trip I made there back in December 1997. I had started learning Serb-Croat in October of that year to complement my Business Management and Russian course in my second year at Durham. I thought that it would enhance my prospects of finding a job. Funnily enough, I now use the Yugoslav language every day for my work here in Luxembourg and I love it. It is so phonetic, so clear, so cool. Greetings are '*Gde si?*' (Where are you?) '*Sta radis?*' (What are you doing?)

Anyway in December 1997, after the first term of my second year at Durham, I felt driven to go to the former Yugoslavia and see for myself what was going on there. I wanted to see the aftermath of a truly terrible war, a very bloody conflict. A chap called Peter Biston, who was two years above me, recommended I read a book called *The Fall of Yugoslavia* by Misha Glenny. I was very excited and had absolutely no fear. John Bisham and I had dropped into Croatia on our travels from Slovakia a year and a half previously. We then witnessed a town destroyed by the war and I wanted to see if there had been any progress there. I sort of justified my trip by saying that I would pop into the embassies in several countries to enquire about employment prospects for my year out the following year. I never did.

I left on 12 December with just $200 in my money belt. I had a small holdall and a few belongings. I also had a booklet of addresses of students who belonged to the European society. This was my security. I would never be stuck, since I had these contacts. I never used them, even though I tried once.

Anyway, on 12 December I hitched from Luxembourg with the goal of being back home for Christmas. I wanted to see Croatia, Bosnia and Serbia and pop in on Slovakia to see my girlfriend, Bianca, on the way home. All my aims were accomplished. As I told my

Yugoslav friend yesterday in Brussels, I hitched from Luxembourg to Zagreb, the capital of Croatia, caught a bus from Zagreb to Split and then Dubrovnik, where I stayed for a few days, before catching the bus from Dubrovnik into Bosnia. I stopped off in the town of Mostar, travelled into or up towards Sarajevo, where I coincidentally met some Bosnian Muslims who gave me a place to stay. I went north to the town of Tuzla with one of them, bussed across the Serbska Republic into Serbia, where I had to do a bit of sweet-talking on the border – they wanted my dollars, which I refused to part with – into Belgrade where I spent just a few hours wandering around. I remember the journey from Bosnia to Belgrade, observing pigs hanging off village houses after the slaughter, then I caught the train from the capital of Serbia to Budapest in Hungary. That train journey, I recall feeling very proud, since I shared a compartment with five Serbians, I think, and we discussed the pros and cons of military service all in Serbian! I had only been learning the language since September! The groundings of my Russian were a real help. I must add, the teaching of it was excellent in Durham, truly excellent, courtesy of a very motherly woman called Mrs Pitter. Furthermore, I have a natural talent or gift, if you like, for picking up foreign languages. My father, Peter, did Greek and Latin at school and my mother Latin, French and some Spanish, so it must be in the genes. I have them to thank.

Neither of my parents went to university but they are both highly intelligent people and surprisingly, perhaps somewhat boring, all four of their children went to Durham University, one after the other.

In Bosnia I saw so much destruction – in Mostar in particular, where the famous bridge was wiped out. What struck me about Bosnia was the beauty of the country, the hills, the mountains, the gorges and the rivers. One of the most beautiful places I have ever been to.

I recall the bus journey from Mostar to Sarajevo – the sense of company on the bus. I was sitting at the back. Everyone was chatting about this and that. Then two or three people lit up when it was obviously forbidden. Nobody cared. I understood that when such a devastating thing as war has happened, smoking on the back of a bus no longer seems important.

I must go; Edin has just called. We have some more work at home in Uselberg. Today we are painting the living room. Today is

Tuesday, 25 January and I still want to recount some more about yesterday's trip to Brussels. All the way home I was thinking about what I wanted to tell you, my friends: some good, positive, thoughtful words, but they will have to wait. See you soon. Cheers.

Hi there! I'm back from work. It's about eleven thirty, and I'm not very tired. How was your day, whoever you are?

My hair, of which there is not much, is covered in white paint. The high point of today was coffee, between painting the ceiling and painting the walls, then dinner when the job was finished at ten o'clock, which consisted of a pizza. One was a tuna and onion and the other four cheeses.

I feel as though I have run out of steam with writing this book; I have lost the inclination. Life is going OK, work is good, we have lots of it. I can build and build my business, employ more Yugoslavs, advertise more.

I have a certain belief that this book will make me famous and, moreover, rich. I don't really care about fame, but a little extra cash wouldn't go amiss. I have so many ideas of what I would spend it on. So, if you have a friend, then please invite him or her to invest in this book. That would be a great help – thanks!

Tomorrow we are finishing off the living room at home. It should take less time than today's job.

I had so much to tell you driving back from Brussels yesterday, so much. My head was full of positive thoughts.

Anyway, what would you like to hear now? I could tell you some more about my past life; the present no longer holds anything of interest, just work.

We could write about families, travel, love, friendships, some more about my humble understanding of who or what God is, a little about life in general, a story or two, or simply a short account of my childhood.

On the way to pick up Edin this morning, I imagined how famous I would be. I imagined the book being published and everyone, the British population that is, flocking to buy it. The book is primarily aimed at the British. If it is translated, that is fine. I imagined making the headlines of every newspaper, then the paparazzi coming to Luxembourg to track me down, then my close friends and family being interviewed. I was thinking how life could change. But would it? I would still go on working as I do. If the paparazzi came, I would simply tell them to go away and get a proper job and stop interfering in other people's lives. I imagined getting radio interviews, perhaps a TV slot? I don't think I would accept. I have work to do, friends to look after, maybe another book to write, which I thought would be a love story. I love my life, my God-given life. I am very happy.

My thoughts coming back from Brussels were that life is so very short. We have no time to lose. To the depressed: pick yourself up, fight for your life, do something positive. Go out of doors, look at the sky, observe nature. Think how lucky you are to be alive, to exist. It is such a coincidence that we exist at all – sperm meets egg. For the lonely: go out and make a friend. Don't be afraid of contact. Be free, and if you have money, spend wisely. Spend it. Do nice things, enjoy your friends, help your friends. If you have the gift to make money, do it, make lots. No need to feel any guilt. You don't know how people in less privileged countries are envious of the life we lead. They would do the same if in our position.

If you have a girlfriend or boyfriend, do nice things together, enjoy one another, go out for walks. If you are a lad, take your bird on a romantic trip somewhere. You don't need much money. Go on a camping trip or go cycling together somewhere. Outdoor trips are the best, I think.

If you smoke or drink, that's fine as long as you are doing something with your life. What's the point of getting wasted on a Friday night and spending the whole of Saturday in bed?

Live for the day and make the most of opportunities. They come thick and fast if you believe, so keep your eyes open. Look around you. Be alert.

To state the obvious, friends are good, so appreciate them and call them. Keep the contact; it is worth it. We can't live this life on our own. We need someone to turn to every now and again.

I lived a very lonely life for years. I isolated myself. That's no good.

Plans are good, but what happens if they fail? We can't look too far ahead because you never know – the Lord can take our lives at a flick of a finger. We can be inflicted with illness. Cancer comes to the best of us.

I have just had a nice conversation with Uta, my girlfriend. She is incredibly understanding. What I mean is that she understands me well. She understands what I say immediately, which is good. I am so lucky to have found her. In fact, it was the other way round – she found me. She saw my advert in the English-speaking newspaper and rang me one Wednesday lunchtime while I was at my Russian lesson. She asked me what I did apart from gardening and I said, 'Most things'. She said, 'Do you drive?' and I answered, 'Yes'. She told me that she had broken her foot and had a child, and asked me if I was good with children.

Hello there, my dear and loyal friends. How much I love you all. Stay with me, please. My time span is running out. I initially told myself twelve days, but I may have to increase it by two. I absolutely need to get this book published. It is my number one priority.

How are you all today? Had a good day? Been up to anything? I hope so, for your sake. Whatever you are up to, keep at it, it is worth it.

I have just had a friend ring me to suggest meeting up. We did and she informed me that soon she is about to do the Trans-Siberian rail trip from Vladivostok to Moscow, but she will first fly to Beijing, take the Trans-Mongolian railway to Lake Baikal, make the trip across Russia (ten time zones, by the way), to Moscow and then the final leg up to St Petersburg and fly back home from there. I was so pleased that she told me, so pleased. So, if any of you have any great plans, do scribble me a note or an email to let me know. I can only encourage you.

I remember in the early stages of my illness when I was really struggling, I badly needed encouragement and someone to tell me that I could do it. Whoever you are, if you are in the same boat, take courage, you *can* do it, whatever it is. Make yourself better; get on with it and live in hope.

I also had a desperate need to talk. I needed someone to listen to what I had to say and I needed someone to review my life. I needed to say, 'This is where I have been, this is where I am at, this is where I want to be.' For such a long time I felt I had no one, no one who would really listen.

All I know is that the help I needed in the early stages was for someone to say, 'Stop. You have time; no need to hurry. Take little steps and build gradually. Do this first, and then you can move on to greater things.' I think I needed a counsellor. The worst feeling is that you are on your own.

After university I felt I was falling and falling into a big, dark, deep pit. I could see the pace at which I was falling and it built up momentum. It was very scary. I needed someone to help me. I felt there was no one around to do so. If you are in that position, seek help fast. Go to a doctor, not a psychiatrist, he will just prescribe you medicine. Try and find someone who will listen, really listen. There are people trained for this. Luxembourg is crap for this but I know that Britain is far better! It is not weak to seek help, absolutely not; pride has nothing to do with it. Forget your principles, forget your pride – just do it. It is written in the Bible: 'Seek and you shall find.' If the first person you go to is no good, then look for someone else. It's the same principle for finding a job: seek and you shall find. Life doesn't come to you, you have to go to it. If you break your leg, you go to a doctor; if you have a headache, you take an aspirin; if you have a cold, you see your GP. It's the same for mental illness: if you are feeling psychologically unstable, seek help, go and sort it out. There is nothing wrong with it and nothing, I stress, nothing, to be embarrassed or ashamed about. There is a stigma attached to mental illness, it is almost taboo. I have many friends now who have supported me one way or another. Get to the root of your problem early before it gets too serious. Don't, whatever you do, wait!

I am saying all this because I want you to avoid going where I have been. It is very dark and very scary and when you've fallen, the effort to get out is tremendous. I have been so low, so mixed up, so lost, so disturbed, so lonely. I have had so many diagnoses – clinical depression, psychosis, and paranoid schizophrenia. I can say this honestly: not one of them have I ever had. I may have suffered symptoms of one or the other, but never have I been psychotic or schizophrenic. These are just labels and we, as humans, can't be labelled. Medicine exists to stop you hearing voices, if that is the case. It also exists to calm your mind. The best medicine, I still believe, for most of these illnesses, is simple one-to-one counselling. Talk it out, whatever you are going through. Be reassured that someone has been there before you. You are not alone or the only one.

Find a doctor who really cares about your welfare or well-being. I hate to say it, but I have been very unlucky here in Luxembourg. Sadly, the majority of the doctors here are in the profession for financial reasons. They are happy to provide some medicine, but very few will really listen.

You are you, you are a person, you are special, you have your thoughts, your ideas, your needs, your desires, your dreams. I believe, as my friend Louisa has recently reiterated, that anyone can suffer mental illness. I have met some truly incredible people inside psychiatric hospitals. 'Get your needs met' is my message to you. It is our busy and hectic society that produces stress and anxiety and depression. I think these are all relatively new illnesses. I am sure in the fifteenth century these didn't exist. It is the sensitive who are the victims, I am afraid. Be strong; do not be afraid. Battle on; don't let people trample on you. Don't let people tell you that you are ill. I hate that word, 'ill'. 'You are ill,' they said. The word condemns you. You are a person; you are a human being. You are precious; your life is a gift.

I had big ideas whilst at university, different ideas. How can medicine sort out your ideas? That is nonsense. I am sorry, but it is. I had ideas of revolution, of changing the world. I still do, and I am still on medication. Ideas are good. They are what make you you, so don't be ashamed of them. Find people who will listen to you, people who will build you up. Avoid people who put you down. Choose your friends well. They say that friends you can choose, family you can't. Family you are born into – you have no choice. You can't always be with family. Sometimes you must leave, release yourself from their grasp. Get out into the world. Meet new people, travel – escape.

Back in November 2002, I was in London and I met up with Hussein, a friend of mine from Durham. He saw me in my miserable state and he told me to be grateful for two things: education and health. That is an advantage we have over many of our fellow men around the world. He told me to travel on my own. He had great plans for his own life. Thank you, Hussein, if you are reading this.

Back to families. Parents will always see you as their child, even when you are grown up. They have great trouble in respecting you as an adult, as an individual. I had great problems with my mother.

She had her own plans for my life. She had an idea of what she wanted me to be, and where she wanted me to be. When I found my belief in what I call God, she couldn't accept the new authority I had. Our characters clashed. I still don't know to this day what she wanted for me. She couldn't accept that I may have had my own plans and ideas for what would make me happy. To this day I still hate her for what she did to me. She is so screwed up; she thinks she is a perfect little angel and she is such a good actress. I don't know anyone who sees the truth about my mother. I haven't found one person who sees what I see. She puts on this show about being so sweet and kind and angelic. She caused me a mountain of distress.

She had her own problems with her father and she has never been prepared to let me go. She doesn't believe in the same God that I believe in, I can see. Maybe she is a Hindu – just kidding. If she did believe in God, like I do, then she would believe in me and be behind me in what I want to be in this life. She has never really been behind me.

I hate that bitch. I really hate her and in my particularly suicidal stage, I could have finished things between us. I really could have. I would have lived in peace knowing that she was out of my world. It would have given me a huge sense of satisfaction. Even if it meant me spending the rest of my life behind bars. I would have been happy.

Now I have to press on and accept that she is still living. What can I do?

She doesn't have the slightest bit of respect for me.

The mother of a girlfriend I had told me in secret one evening what she thought about my mother. She asked me if I really wanted to know and I said, 'Yes.' 'Your mother' (I will try and get it right) 'is incredibly selfish, thoroughly stupid and very, very spoilt.' There we go – one person on my side. That makes me feel a whole world better.

I always went to the psychiatrist in the early stages, not for my sake but for my mother's. I thought I could keep her happy. I sort of thought that I would suffer for her; I thought maybe something would change with her. To this day she is just the same. I can see the truth now. I was never ill. It was she who needed help. What an idiot! What an absolute farce!

I am really worried now because you may think I have lost it. I am worried that you think that I am ill. What can I say? I am simply telling you a bit about my life and my experience of psychiatry. Maybe my mother will never change. That is her problem, her loss. Maybe she will never respect me or love me as a fellow Christian. She laughs at me, doesn't listen to a word I tell her. It says in Corinthians 13, the passage about love, 'And you may have a faith as big as mountains, but without love it is nothing', so, now I simply go on loving her and forgiving her and praying to the Almighty that one day she may come to her senses and grow up, like I told the Americans to do.

Jules at Rijeka, Croatia – whilst on a hitch!

Jules with Slovak pupils

Jordan, April 2000, 'Ordered'

Not given in as yet

Marta

Raffles – the master of all canines! – alas, no longer with us.

Jules' family

Jules flip-flopping in the Maekong

In Moscow – the Red Square

With Year 1 Muscovite students of English, Moscow

The Bolshoi Theatre

*With the beauties in Russia – school children raising 'toasts'
(So nice compared to their English counterparts!)*

Lake in Elektrostal, Russia – Haven of peace

Temporarily suspended bridge, Mostar, Bosnia, 1997

Jules in his element

Four Durham students en route for Elektrostal, a provincial town beyond Moscow

Jules' parents' residence in Luxembourg – Shine, Jesus! Shine!

Enjoying the affection of a lion cub, South Africa, 1997

Streaking on ice! Calgary, Canada, 1998

Jules and Edin taking a break

Jules in 2004 – the world will come to its fruition

Chapter Five

Wow! I am glad that chapter is over. I have got a lot off my chest.

I have been in a psychiatric ward a total of seven times, six of them in Luxembourg, once in Vienna. That was the best experience, but I didn't enjoy it. I always wanted out. The first time in December 2000. I was in a psychiatric ward of the Centre Hospitalier for two months. In that short period of time I managed to escape from a closed ward seven times. But I have never believed in escaping from your problems, so I always came back. They say that you take your problems with you, even if you change environment. That is very true.

I have never suited psychiatry; it is bullshit. Lying in your bed, waiting for the nurses to bring you medicine, doing nothing. They offer various therapies with gymnastics in the morning, and a walk in the afternoon around the hospital grounds.

I knew I never needed medicine. All I needed was TLC (tender loving care) and a rest, ideally in a monastery. The love, ultimately, from a girlfriend, since I didn't get it from my mother. She struggled with the concept of loving. Is that fair? So many of us think we would like some time out, but where or how? I mean a prolonged time out, not simply a one or two week holiday.

If I had received good, Christian love from my mother, I never would have had problems. I always had something to prove. I always wanted to get away from home.

Someone very special came into my life post-university; her name is Simmy, for short. In the summer of 2000, after graduating from Durham, I received a postcard from Turkey signed 'Sim'. Her last phrase was, 'I can see you baking your bread.' I will tell you what that meant later. I couldn't, for a moment, think who she was. I soon wrote back to her thanking her for the postcard and admitting that I didn't know who she was. Then, one day, it clicked – I remembered. An Edwardian-style relationship began. For the first six months simply sending each other letters. I remember her telling me not to lose her because of my spirituality. I promised her I wouldn't. This girl was gorgeous, she had a real aura, a sense of purpose and most importantly, she looked good, with dark hair and freckles. She was half-Peruvian, half-English. I invited her to Luxembourg.

Wait! I wanted to slag my mother off a bit more. Every six months she goes off on those expensive trips to the mountains and nice places and she comes back to her home comforts and her life never changes. She boasts of the heights she has reached and things she has learned, but she spends her whole life with privileged people. If she were a true Christian, which she claims to be, then she would walk with simple people and share her God-given life with them, too. She has a stupid routine at home, writes letters to all the family on the computer on a Monday morning, doesn't clean the house herself because she employs a Yugoslavian girl, walks a lot and spends the rest of the time with her feet up reading the *Daily Telegraph* cover to cover. I know her routine because I have lived at home with her for months. She has no life.

And now, you know what she is doing? She is doing a first-aid course because it makes her feel good. When will she use it? On her walks in the stupid mountains? There are all sorts of clubs she could join – the British Ladies' Club, for example – but she puts herself above other women. She thinks she is better than them. Her one good quality is that she has a sense of humour and a good sense of fun; she never takes life too seriously.

I have always wanted her to be a perfect and loyal housewife and mother, serving the Lord at home, working at raising her family with love but she has always resented this role. She just doesn't understand. Or maybe she is a rebel.

My dear readers, bear with me. I have a few more things to say. It is very cold here in Luxembourg, the ground is frozen, it is about -5° C, but the sky is clear, the stars are out in abundance and the glorious moon is shining. I have drunk two packet soups, several glasses of milk and one coffee and have smoked half a dozen cigarettes – bad, I know. I have just spoken to Uta on the phone.

Simmy and I finally met up at Easter time year 2001 after eight months of letter-writing. She flew to Luxembourg and I went to the airport in my old man's Volkswagen camper with a trailer. On the way, I bought her some red tulips from a flower shop. I was very nervous. When I saw her, she looked better than I remembered.

That night in my flat, she slept in my room. The next day we went on a long trip to a place called Vianden in the north of Luxembourg to visit an extremely inspiring castle. On entering Vianden, we stopped in front of a church and we kissed for the first time in the graveyard.

Three days later, after Easter, I took her back to the airport and she asked me if I would come to her birthday party in Durham in June – she was in her final year at Durham University. I replied, 'Lord willing!' She really didn't like that. How could I know? In retrospect I wasn't ready for a serious relationship, but I kept it going. I began to love her more and more. I remember proposing to her in the garden during the summer, whilst we were doing some planting in the garden. She sort of said yes, but added only when I was better and off my medication. She was the third girl I had proposed to. I was still a long way from being well. I realise now that I couldn't get better for her, or for her sake. I had to do it for myself, which I have now more or less succeeded in doing. Praise be to myself.

I am now feeling guilty about what I have written about my mother. She is a lovely woman, very sweet-hearted and generous, always trying to do her best. I believe I am the only person who can really help her, but first it has been important that I help myself and continue to strive to be well. Thanks to the conversation I have just had with Uta, I believe that is why my mother, Ann-Marie, was so adamant and forthcoming about putting me through psychiatry. In her opinion, I need to get myself better, so that, ultimately, I can help her. Basically, my mother projects her life on to mine and my siblings.

However, when I am alone with her, I can't help attacking her. As a result she persistently has her defences up.

My father, Peter, is so humble and kind. He is incredibly patient. Just this evening he had his father on the phone, talking him through how to use the computer. The conversation went on for ever. My grandpa, Sam Richard Vaudrey, lives in Fordingbridge in Hampshire and should go on for a long time yet. He is eighty-eight years old and an incredibly determined old man. He is a conservative and has very admirable values. He is always up for serious conversation about politics and Europe at the dinner table. His wife, Eve, died in her sleep about eight years ago. Grandpa recently went on a cruise to Greenland and Iceland, which he enjoyed very much. I have stayed with him on several occasions in the last six months. He has researched our family tree and is determined to keep to traditions. My mother had many problems with him and always resented making him a cooked breakfast. If that's what he likes, why not? My Durham friends, Nicholas and James, loved him. They thought he was very old school. He and his wife came to stay with us in our student house in Durham, which was very game of them. Whenever I see him, he always thanks me for that occasion and states that he had a lot of fun.

Are you interested in my family? It is better than talking about myself the whole time.

My mother is an excellent worker, a perfectionist like me, and a sound gardener. She has a passion for the mountains and the outdoors. She has a keen vision of what she likes. She is a fighter and believes in doing what is right, very law-abiding. She has brought me and my two brothers and my sister up in a very rigid way: to have polite manners, sit up straight at the table and to never take drugs, which none of us have ever done, thank God. When we were all young, after school she drove us all around to our various activities: piano, rugger and riding. She used to cook lunch for us in the camper van. I think now that she believes she deserves the rest she is having, having worked hard for so many years, flying around the place, primarily chasing her husband. Mother used to work for the Foreign Office in Beirut and then Brussels. She had a boyfriend called Dick who used to take her skiing and other romantic things. He, I think, was my mother's real love.

I can go on and on about my friends, family and travels and personal experience, but how much should I write?

Tomorrow, first thing, if I get up in time, I am going to drop in on my good pal, Billy, whom I always insult on the dog and bone. He is an artist, a graphic designer and he aspires to be famous one day. He is already fairly well known here in Luxembourg. He is always up early in the morning, sorting out one thing or another, and paints all day long. He churns out a lot of work; presently his theme is steel work, which he is exhibiting in a place called Esch.

He has had several exhibitions and he does commissions for people. Recently he had some of his work printed on silk scarves and ties. He is known to be a bit arrogant and up himself, somewhat poncey, but deep down he is such a good person. He has been my most faithful friend over the last few years, always by my side and it is he who telephoned to suggest we meet tomorrow. We always have a good heart-to-heart, never too serious; we always have plenty to tell each other. We are both interested in one another's lives. He will always do very well. His best attribute is his discipline and thoroughness. He has a lovely girlfriend called Romana. She is from Mexico, and is half-Mexican, half-German. The last time I saw him, I told him that I would help him become famous. Maybe the tables have turned?

I am a Christian and I have a calling; I need to take life more seriously.

From now until I reach heaven I am going to live and learn. I would like to discover more truths about our God. I would like to have a thorough understanding of the Scriptures. I would like to be able to quote more verses from them. If I can back up my belief system with concrete knowledge of the Bible, then I may one day start talking some sense. The Bible is so full of juicy stuff – I love it, especially the letters to Paul. Christianity can flourish again as it once did, but I think it is dormant for the time being, in this present day and age.

Yesterday, Edin and I finished painting the living room and the piano room, both a magnolia colour. They look great. Today we are working on the floor. The task involves pulling up the carpet and then sanding away the glue that had held it down. For this we need to hire a machine. But first I have to see my friend, Billy. He is so brilliant, always full of energy and on the ball.

All the best, my friends. I will have to bring my writing to a close in a day or two, so I will try and write a lot tonight. I acknowledge that some, or much, of what I have written is contradictory, but bear with me. It has been a stream of consciousness. I hope you have enjoyed it. See you soon. J.

Don't forget to say your prayers. If you ask for something according to the will of God, then He will answer. God is bountiful in His love for us. He adores us, I know it. Cheerio, have fun today.

Hi! Today is Friday – one more day of hard work. Yesterday we worked from eleven through until ten in the evening.

Wahey! What's up? Life is plodding on. Susannah, my sister, can feel kicks in her stomach – it's exciting for her. If you don't know, she is pregnant. She was asking how to remove wallpaper. They are looking at new houses at the moment. They live in Wokingham.

Life is difficult sometimes. I was just cooking scrambled eggs and the first egg I cracked fell all over the counter. Why? I thought. I don't need this. The eggs – only two left – were good nevertheless. That's all I have eaten today and I didn't get round to eating last night. On the way home, after a crazy night out on the razzle, I stopped off at a hotel for one last drink, and also in the hope of pulling. What I did was gatecrash an Icelandic party! Three hundred of them, all having a whale of a time. Drinking, sitting around tables, dancing. I spotted two girls, one blonde, one dark-haired, sitting at a table. The blonde girl, I forget her name, immediately sent me to the dance floor and instructed me to look a girl in the eyes and boogie away. She informed me that there were plenty of single girls. I tried but didn't have much luck. I preferred just sitting at the table with a beer and chatting. I went straight back to the blonde and told her that I thought she was the most beautiful of all the girls.

Chapter Six

The cleaning – I have just done most of it myself. I have spent too long waiting for someone else to do it. A guy like me who spends all day, every day, working physically should be able to push a Hoover around his flat. All that remains is the washing-up. It humbles you somewhat. Who are we to think we are above menial tasks like these? However 'important' you are, get down on your hands and knees and do some scrubbing!

Many Luxembourgers employ Portuguese people to do their housework. I hope one day that the Portuguese here in Luxembourg will be repatriated. They work so hard and they deserve to go back to their own country. All the roads have nearly been dug and most of the Luxo houses are clean.

I believe in repatriation. I don't believe in leaving your home country looking for a better life elsewhere. We have nationality and we have culture. They say that in two generations the Luxembourgish language will no longer exist. This is a really sad loss of culture and many Luxembourgers are trying hard to hold on to it. But there is so much intermarriage. Forty per cent of the Luxembourg population is foreign. Luxembourg has the highest per capita standard of living and income in the world. And, as I gathered from a conversation on Saturday night, the younger generation are trying to outdo their parents. All the young go to Brussels, Paris and Munich to study, then return here and 'get a good job' – architect, lawyer, politician, teacher.

I had so many difficulties when I was looking for work in this country. I was so humiliated. I hated looking for a nine-to-five job, but I was encouraged to do so. I have never believed in going to a job centre to look for a job. Links, contacts, friends. Your network. Going to a centre and filling out a form made me feel as though I were nothing. There is absolutely no personal connection. I also have a problem with CVs. Everyone, as I understand it, joins in extra-curricular activities at school and university so that they will look good on their CV. What suckers! People aren't doing things for themselves. They are doing things for prospective employers.

Following the way of the system. The hold of society is so incredibly strong. We are all so indoctrinated.

I have just returned from a cabaret. I had a lot of fun. Actually, I didn't really. It was a waste of time. I believe contact between a man and a woman has to lead somewhere. I don't believe platonic relationships are possible. There is always one of the two who fancies the other. Cabaret girls, in fancy clubs with nice decorations and dimmed lights, spend their nights chatting up lonely guys, like myself, with the sole aim of enticing them to drink, and perhaps buy one for them as well. They receive commission on every drink that is bought for them. They make themselves look beautiful, dress elegantly and look after these boring, desperate guys. They are wasting so much time; they could be looking for a guy with whom to develop a loving relationship.

Why do I go to such places? Good question. I like the atmosphere. I like the ease at which these girls approach me, even if I know that they are just trying to entice me to buy drinks. I often enjoy their stories, and it's a good alternative to Luxo bars and clubs where the music scene is bad. In those places, there is absolutely no opportunity to speak to anyone, as the music is too loud. The gentlemen and ladies are relatively stuck-up and remain in large groups. What can you do? I always want to go home and ring my girlfriend, Uta, but I get stuck in town. I go from bar to bar looking for something, I don't know what. The nightlife in Luxland is awful, although I used to consider it good.

Hi guys. Back from the razzle. I'm back in business, relatively speaking. Work has quickened. We had a big job last week, which took up a lot of time, but I try not to let anything get me down.

I rang my friend Jim Warrior last night, a housemate from Durham. He sounded genuinely pleased to hear from me. He was in Courcheval skiing. He expressed concern about my health and told me that he had various reports from several different sources about what had been going on with me over the last few years. He claimed he simply didn't know how to act or respond towards me. I shall see him, Lord willing, in a month or so.

Right now, I am living an incredible life. Life is continually on the up. I am learning stuff at an exponential level – my learning ability is one of my assets. I am very sharp and do not miss a thing. I accept my own ignorance, which helps me learn more. People who think they know everything already are talking bullshit. When I don't know something, I ask questions. I was teased at Rugby School for asking too many questions. Why this? Why that? 'Here's Julian Vaudrey – it's question time,' my pals would say – or should I call them associates?

What am I learning? Lots of things. How to run a business. How to do your best to keep your workers happy. How to earn and retain respect. How to be with clients. I ask myself whether I should keep my business small or whether I should develop it. There are endless possibilities for the latter: employ more guys, buy some office space, purchase more vehicles, employ a secretary, employ a marketing manager. As I understand it, to develop a business you need a vision. If you have a vision and if you can to share your vision, then those around you are happier. Clients see it, your workers see it, your friends, your family. I think it radiates from you. This vision I don't really have.

What I do have is ideas. At the moment I am juggling these ideas, but biding my time. I don't wish to move too fast, take steps that are too big. I have time. Then there is, of course, finance. Who pays? Generally, at the moment, I am putting all earnings straight back into the business, buying new equipment and products. One of my principles is to meet demand. If there is demand then I will strive to meet it. I would like to get jobs done as they come in. I would like a reputation for swiftly meeting demand and having everything planned out, not backlogging jobs for months. At the moment, the demand isn't there, but this can change, I am sure. I can instigate this at the click of my fingers, and change things. I have always believed in the market in Luxembourg. There is so much property; there are so many gardens. I can milk this country if I want to. I sell my name; I know the trade both in painting and gardens, having done both. I am a very thorough weeder and I have a very steady hand for painting. I consider myself an expert painter and an expert gardener, and I have plenty of referees who can vouch for this. On top of this, I have a good business mind and am a natural entrepreneur, as evidenced from my childhood. (I will explain later, not now.) Furthermore, I studied business management at university, basic management principles, including the difference between managing and leading, accounting, and marketing. We did a project on WF Electrics to discuss why they had such a big turnover of staff. We worked in a team of four.

We also learnt all about management in organisations, small and medium-sized businesses, management in the Pacific Rim, particularly Japan and China's emerging economy. We touched on the subject of creative management and in the final year, international business and strategy. Most of the latter I found irrelevant – it was too complicated and badly taught. Most stuff you learn about business and management is common sense.

It was the management in organisations that saved my soul and inspired me towards what I am doing now. Funny! Most people studying management at Durham were undertaking it to enhance their chances of success within organisations. The percentage of business management graduates from Durham who go on to work for an international firm must be very high. I met just one guy who stood out from the rest. We met for coffee one afternoon after lectures and he told me that antiques was his thing. He had an uncle who ran an antiques business that he wished to take over. He was a very energetic guy and I was particularly impressed by his ability to run Tai Chi classes.

Chapter Seven

More about mental illness. We are now into February and time is pressing on. The other evening I boasted to a guy older than myself that I thought my age, twenty-eight, was still young. I don't really believe this is true. Do you peak at a certain age and then decline? Surely life gets better as you get older and wiser? I have met so many middle-aged people who love their age, their maturity, their ability to discover new things; who are happy in their marriages or happier now divorced.

I want to tell you about the cat and the mouse that I chanced upon on walking out of my apartment yesterday. The cat was in hot pursuit of the mouse, who, in terror, was scrambling for his life. I didn't feel pity for the mouse until later on in the car. The mouse was so minute, and, in comparison, the cat was a giant. Predators and victims – that's what nature is all about, isn't it? The life cycle. We learnt all about this in biology classes. My parents' cleaner, Asila, a Yugoslav girl, who I met yesterday whilst at home painting the radiator, told me that mice can be real pests.

After work yesterday, I went to see the film, *Sideways*, a film about two college mates who venture out on a week-long holiday together before one of them is to marry. Jack is determined to have a last minute affair whilst away; he is very worried about the life-long commitment he was about to undertake. He mentions, maybe jokingly or ironically, that this was his 'last week of freedom.'

Permit me to express my opinion. I don't believe marriage is a curbing of one's freedom or liberty. You can be equally free in a relationship or out. Love shouldn't be possessive or demanding or selfish or restricting. I believe that when you are married you should be more free to do as you choose. The difference is that you may not want to go out until one in the morning every night like you used to, because you actually want to be with your loving and adorable wife.

I am meant to be scribbling a few more words about mental illness, not about marriage, relationships or love affairs and cheating. More on that subject later.

I just met a guy in the pub who informed me that where you are from or what you believe in is not important. So I asked him, 'What is? What matters?' He replied that all that matters is you believe in something or anything, most importantly in yourself. I have heard this before, and I agree with him. Self-belief is important. I have also heard people say that they believe in their family and their friends. You know by now, I am sure, that I believe in God, but I would very much like to reiterate that that is the last thing I am advocating. I have found God, and the last thing I am saying is that you should. Life is a journey; we all make discoveries along the way. We experience enlightenment, we have realisations, we have dreams, and some or most of us experience the mystical at some or other stage of our lives.

On having faith in oneself – I, personally, am trying. I know what it means to completely lose self-belief, to think that all you have done has failed, that you are a loser like the chap in the film last night, to focus on the negative. Ultimately, I would like to say that I do believe in myself. But the truth is – not completely. I still don't know myself fully. When does one? I am discovering stuff about myself every day. I know I always underestimate myself. So I often surprise myself.

I have always believed in God, however. I know that God is real. I have 100 per cent belief in Him. God will never let you down; he is always there. Jesus is the best friend you will ever have. No friend is 100 per cent loyal or faithful, but I am proud to be able to claim that God is sure. He is 100 per cent. He is.

What I have just been writing about leads me to so many issues. Self-love, self-respect, self-confidence. The next person I meet who tells me that he believes in himself, I will ask, 'Who are you? What can you do? Do you really know yourself? What are your gifts, your talents, your capabilities? What are you capable of? How far have you pushed yourself? Have you ever suffered? Do you know your limits?'

Now I can safely claim that I pretty much can answer all these questions for myself. I know when I am tired, unhappy or depressed. I know when I am angry, anxious or worried. I know when I pity myself. I know when I am boring someone. I remember going to a 'glimpse' weekend with the Right Hand Trust, a Christian organisation in Wales at the end of my time at Durham. I was looking for something to grasp on to or focus my energies on after my disastrous split with Marta (who I discuss in Chapter One). At this 'glimpse' weekend we were split into pairs and asked to ask each other what our strengths and weaknesses were. I was really put on the spot. I simply didn't know. I didn't know myself. Strengths I could easily list, but I didn't think I had any weaknesses. We all do, of course. In a reference letter, in application for a placement with the same charity, my aunt/godmother wrote that my biggest weakness was that I didn't know my strengths. Perhaps this is one of my weaknesses, but others I have come to accept are that my concentration span is weak; I am easily distracted; I am easily led astray; I am easily tempted; I am not very strong-minded; I have an aptitude for being lazy (I have my father to thank there) and I tend to take things for granted; I don't easily appreciate what I have; I am never satisfied with the status quo; I always want more. Am I alone? I have about half a century to realise my full potential.

I am extremely disorganised, a little bit scatty, and not always on the ball. I still don't have a wallet, no watch and no bank account. My pockets are always filled with all sorts of things. I like to have cash in my pockets; I take no interest in time. I am not time-obsessed. I have an alarm clock beside my bed and a clock in the car. Elsewhere, I simply stop and ask someone. If you, I believe, are always watching the clock, time will never pass. These days I don't ever want time to pass. There is never enough of it. I have so much to do and so little time. They say (you have probably heard this before), 'If you want something done, ask a busy person.'

Let me tell you about this morning. After going with Edin to receive payment for the flat we decorated last week, I went to the English language newspaper office called *352*, the first area digit of the dialling code for Luxembourg, the paper in which I advertise, and I wished to have a few words with the editor, a girl called Miss Barnsley – a lovely, very pleasant girl who I met in the pub the other night at Bert's leaving drinks.

On asking her if she had a couple of minutes to chat, I bumped my head against the door. She said, 'Oh, watch your head!'

I, ironically, enjoy it when things like that happen in a lady's presence because it humbles you and then, I believe, the girl in question likes you more. That has happened to me on more than one occasion.

Anyway, she made the conversation relatively easy. I was extremely nervous. I could feel myself trembling all over and my heart was beating at a rate of – can I remember the expression? – half a dozen something… I said goodbye and told her I would see her soon.

On Sunday I went to the psychiatric hospital, where I had spent two months in the summer of 2002. The guy I met shocked me, and since then I have thought a lot about my own experiences there. It was a special sojourn.

I believe God filled the ward with some fascinating people of all shapes and sizes. On the whole we had a good time, but we all felt like animals locked up in a cage. We were badly looked after, treated with extreme disrespect and spoon-fed a whole cocktail of nasty medicine. We smoked together, chatted in the passageways, sat glued to the TV. I was almost beaten up on the first day by a couple of Yugos until they disappeared. I had various admirers. One, a Luxembourgish girl called Carol, was very charming, but I could never quite keep her happy. Then an older girl called Angel who arrived very disturbed, claiming to have had written letters to Blair and Bush. She was an avid freedom fighter. She told me that if I really wanted to get out, I would be able to. I proposed to her; a fellow inmate, who claimed to have studied theology, was going to marry us. We very nearly made love, but she said we should wait until we were out. We exchanged addresses, one of which was that of a farm in France. One day she wore a very beautiful, flowery dress.

I did my utmost to run away from that place. I even tried to smash the windows at the back with a table. The glass was plastic – a slight contradiction, I know. The trouble was that every time I tried to get out, I lost faith and despaired of having the effort required to build it back up again. So the process went on and on. They told my sister, when she came, that I was a very powerful guy.

After two months of this nonsense I was set free. But I had lost all drive, hope and ambition. I was a broken, despairing and lost guy. I felt that, for my own sense of pride, I had to escape by my own means. I succeeded once, but was so lost that, when found, I easily succumbed to going back. I had nowhere to go. Absolutely nowhere. I discovered halfway thorough my sojourn there that it was my parents who had placed me in that psychiatric prison, not the police. This meant that they indeed had the power to lift the placement at their liberty. The trouble was that until then I had absolutely no trust with my father. I pleaded with him on the phone, day after day, to come and lift the placement, but he refused outright. I could sense his fear. He didn't have the guts. I lost so much respect for him, so much. He was my one hope after I discovered I couldn't release myself. To this day, I still don't know what his hopes were for me or what the foundation of his fear was. What a coward. I knew myself that after only a few weeks I had got better, I had improved. I can understand now, not from the medicine, but from the contact with other people. Maybe it was a combination. Who knows?

The worst thing about it was that I could see my fate slipping away. Friends that I had there improved and left, but I remained. It was awful. The doctor only came in every three days and there was a whole process for being *elargi*, as they called it. First of all a visit to the cafeteria, then an afternoon, then a weekend, then this, then this, then that. It was endless and I couldn't bear it. I understood this and didn't want to go through the said process. I wanted quicker results. I spoke to friends on the phone; I kept having to ask for money from fellow inmates. I remember one conversation with Barry, my mate, who is leaving for Australia in a couple of days, and telling him that I hoped to go to Ibiza. He is a simple guy and purely concentrates on the positive. He expects me to be equally positive and fails to understand when I am not. I have, to this day, to be grateful to this mate, Bert Wilden. A very loyal friend.

God gave me many chances to escape – many. A couple of visits to see the psychologist, Mr Weber. On leaving his office I noticed that the lift to the ground floor was open. A quick dash across the landing and I could have been away and free. Oh what regrets afterwards! If I had got away, I have no idea where I would have gone. I have virtually no mates in Luxembourg who would have accepted me as I was, sat me down, listened to my hopes and fears and encouraged me accordingly. Going to England was no longer an option like it had been during the previous hospital experience. Simmy no longer had any time for me, I know. She simply considered that I was forever blaming my behaviour on my illness and getting away with it. Where were my friends when I most needed them? It was all very well coming to visit me in the hospital, that was easy. But when I escaped and came to them, they immediately closed the door. What cowardly behaviour. Self-satisfied shitheads! I tried on several occasions to put trust in my family, my parents, my brother. To no avail. Scared – that is what they were. Purely scared. I was not suffering from anything scary, nothing very unusual – a slight loss of reality. My friends, your job is to talk me back into an understanding of the real world. Don't run away. Talk to me; speak sense to me. I am sure you are capable of that.

On a recent trip to the UK, I had a really good and fulfilling time, as I generally do when I travel abroad, doing something for myself. Then on return I got depressed again because I couldn't think of one place to go in Luxembourg. I have lived in this damned stupid country for twenty-five years. Not even in my own home I do feel accepted. No one to go to and to talk things through with. This is the reason over the past five or six years for the constant urge in me to leave Luxembourg. In retrospect, I could have made the journey back to Slovakia or Moscow, but who, when feeling lonely and depressed would have the guts to make a journey like that with the possibility, even there, of being rejected. That's what I loathe most: rejection. I have learnt that there are very, very few people in this world on whom you can rely. Very sad, isn't it? Before, I thought I had so many friends, so many contacts, such a large network. But, alas, I was wrong.

One word of encouragement, or something for you to think about. If you have friends, let them know that whatever happens to them or whatever they may go through, you will be there for them, by their side. This is crucial. We all need friends, every single one of us.

I think in Moscow in 1998/99 I may have had a premonition of what was coming. I tried so hard to sustain friendships with both Marta and Randy. In the end I lost Randy to Natasha, his Russian girlfriend; then I lost Marta after our holiday in Tenerife. That is why I don't believe in friendships between men and women. She must have fancied me all along, hoping that one day our friendship would blossom into a relationship. Then after Tenerife, she left me by the wayside – dumped me like a sack cloth off the side of a ship. She had no idea what she was doing to me. Or maybe she did but felt she had every reason to. I have no idea. She has, to this day, never really apologised. Need she have? I loved that girl so much: I looked after her throughout our time in Moscow, picking her up daily from the university where she worked, accompanying her home to the flat. The same in Durham in our final year. I would walk her home from lectures, take her home from the pub she worked in and try to discourage her from continuing to work there, because I could see that such a place wasn't good for a girl like her. She just ignored me, the stubborn girl. And then, I have to say it, all she wanted from me in Tenerife was sex! Can that be true? Have me on her terms and corrupt me. I had hopes of marriage or securing a future with her; I wanted to preserve a belief of mine about no sex before marriage with long-term interests in mind.

Maybe I now have her to thank, because what a boring life I would have led if we had got married and not been sexually active before. Where would we be now? Maybe the revolution I have always dreamed of might have worked. Certainly, we would have returned to Moscow. My plan was for us to live six months in Russia and six months in Luxembourg. Winter months, which I love, in Moscow, and the summer months would be spent looking after my parent's garden in Luxembourg. We would spend summers living in a small hut, refuelling for the gruelling and harsh winter months to come. Living it up for half a year and slumming it for the other. I know it would have worked. I loved that girl. I have always believed in perfect love. I had great plans for Marta and me, but I screwed up in Tenerife and had sex with her. She would have been on her knees if we hadn't. Maybe that wasn't God's plan for our lives. What can I say now? I believe in destiny. I believe that God knows best.

Uta and Kimmy are returning in a few hours. I want to be ready for them. I will be. My head is turning a bit. I haven't taken my medicine for a while.

I love Uta and I love Kimmy. Kimmy is part of the package. I love them equally. They have been in Istanbul for the past three and a half weeks. Now they are coming home. Uta tells me that Istanbul is snowed under, so there is a possibility that they will be delayed. I don't care. I will camp at the airport if I have to, to wait for them.

Uta and I have spoken every day on the phone. I haven't been entirely faithful to her, but I have tried my best. She knows, both the former and the latter. I am convinced I still have her love.

I have enjoyed writing this story. Thank you for listening.

Cheers, big ears and long live the revolution!

Look out for me!

Epilogue

This book has been a stream of consciousness. I have really enjoyed writing it. It has all come out just as it is. Very little has been corrected or altered.

I smoke, but I don't advocate smoking. It certainly isn't cool and is extremely harmful to oneself and to those around you. But I have to add that it has helped me with my writing. It has calmed my nerves when I've felt stressed and has given me an excuse to take breaks.

The book is primarily aimed at the British population, but if it sells across the pond or further abroad, all the better. It will only make me richer. I am a generous person, so I will spend the proceeds wisely.

I have tried to include something for everybody in this novel, drawing on my own experiences to encourage you in whatever way needed. I hope I haven't been condescending at all, or stated the obvious too much. I didn't mention anything about fat people or the elderly or the homeless, although I feel that in one way or another I can relate to all three.

I am not fat, but I have lived through a very self-destructive phase. Furthermore, my girlfriend, Uta, used to be fat but lost 27 kg in six months. It can be done with a little bit of willpower and determination, and by telling yourself that you can and will do it. For example, I will try to lose 5 kg over the next three months. Now that I have set a specific goal, it will be easier.

The elderly. I listened to a brilliant sermon on Sunday in church given by the Reverend Chris Lyon. Chris used to work in a hospice and met many people who were on the verge of passing away. He met several people who had reached a realisation that their end was near and they had accepted this and were content as a result. They would ring him and tell him they had absolutely no worries and were at peace. There is no point living with regret of the past. The past, I am afraid, you cannot change. Nor can you change the fact that you are going to die. That is every man's fate. Have no fear, God will take you into his loving arms and embrace you tight and look after you for eternity. How wonderful is that! Not everyone agrees. One girl, called Danielle, who I met recently, told me that she hoped that when she died everything would be over. She didn't want to live for ever.

The homeless. What can I say? I have slept on the streets on three occasions: once in Paris, once in London and once in Bratislava. I was forced to be homeless. It was not fun. The difference between those who are truly homeless and me is that mine was just a temporary experience for me. It was cold; I was hungry; I was pretty miserable. I had absolutely no belongings and had to beg for food, at least, I tried to, but I found it humiliating. If the people knew what a privileged background I had – public school education, university degree, etc. – they would say, 'But are you not wasting your gifts and talents simply wandering around begging for your living? Did God not give you hands to work with?'

Furthermore, the act of begging annoys people. You play on the consciences of good and kind people. People can't give you everything they have. And people in this modern society are very busy, especially in London. I have been there many times. People are reluctant to finance a smoking and drinking habit or, even worse, drugs. If you are on the latter, get off them. There is help everywhere – you just need to ask for it. Do it, please. Bit by bit, you can sort your life out. There are many success stories around. Don't give up hope. Don't give up. It is humiliating living on the streets. You suffer a serious loss of self-esteem as people scorn you and that is not good. Look for some work, even if that involves washing up in a pub somewhere. Make the effort.

I have done a lot of begging and it is not difficult to do if you are dressed smart and are eloquently spoken. If you come straight out with what you want, then people will give. No one likes to hear a sob story. My brother and I tried that in Rome.

Travelling through Belgium trying to get to England years ago, I was dragged off the train by some Belgian cops for not having a ticket. The cop treated me very roughly. He had every right to do so. In his office, he came straight out with it: 'Get a life! Find a job, find a girlfriend, get some money in your pocket.' That shook me up a bit. Sometimes you need someone to tell you this.

God put me through psychiatry and I couldn't accept it for a long time, hence I tried to escape so many times. But I realise now

I had things to learn. When wanting to escape, God helped me. I believed I could find my way on my own.

Let God guide you through a difficult patch. Trust Him. Trust that He knows what He is doing. Accept. Accept. Accept. Forgive yourself when you feel you have screwed up. Don't look back – it is a serious waste of time. Look forward and be positive. Make plans and try to realise them. Set yourself goals and objectives. Take small steps. For example, this week I will go on two short walks and ring one friend, or I will make three job applications. Be realistic and be fair to yourself. Get help to make these steps.

There is the example of two pairs of footprints on the beach. You are walking side by side with Jesus and then there is just one pair for a while. You ask, 'Why? What happened to Jesus when I most needed him?' The answer, I have been given and assured of, is that that is when he picked you up and carried you in His arms.

To all you girls and ladies out there, keep yourselves looking beautiful. We lads love beautiful ladies. We are not interested in your salary and success. What society dictates is a load of pigswill. Follow your instincts. Man is the breadwinner; you have children to bear. How can you juggle a high-paid job with having children?

This feminist movement – who cares? What are you trying to prove? We gentlemen love to open doors for you and help you put on your jackets and invite you for a drink and take you to the cinema or theatre. Let us be men and play our role, and you can play yours.

Acknowledgements

I would like to thank my sister, Sarah, and her husband, Gary, for accommodating me so often in their home in Wokingham. Good luck with your baby.

My mother, Anna, for preventing me from leaving Luxembourg after university, for locking the doors of our house, for taking and hiding my passport and lastly, most importantly, for putting me into a psychiatric ward when I most needed it.

I thank my father, Peter, for doing the same, not to the same extent, but most importantly for reiterating my need to simply have faith. I thank him for driving all the way to Vienna to pick me up. My brothers, Rab and Kim, who supported me right to the end: always there, always solid, always faithful even at the worst times, always accepting me as Jules, not a schizophrenic, not a manic depressive.

My good friends and pals here in Luxembourg: Billy, Ben Andrews, William Overstall and Tom Edmonston-Low and Charles Heal. The Sibson family, Chris, Ruth and Robert – Rob for telling me that I would be back with the rest of them in no time at all. Ruth for the constant prayerful support.

My Yugoslav friends – the Aiderpassich family, Nuro, Alten, Mirsad and their mother. Alten for always looking so pretty and being a pillar of strength and stability; Kemal, her brother, who was in the ward with me. I hope he is well now. Nuro was a soul mate and we kept each other company in my parents' garden. We both adored and respected the late Raffles, an intelligent sheepdog with attitude.

Patricia (Lady) Heal who persistently came to visit me in the various hospitals and filled me in on her family gossip and the goings-on in Luxembourg.

Peter Faure, a fellow sufferer, who was on the ward week in, week out. Following his visits, I had restored hope that I would reach the top again.

Century, the book of photographs, which kept me occupied in the long and boring days.

The chaplain, Clifford Poole and his wife Jean, for their visits. We shared communion together, which left me upset.

The Bond family for their visit on Christmas day.

Ann Overstall for a jolly sense of fun which lifted my spirit and for all the work she has given me from the kindness of her heart. She has trusted me to paint her kitchen and her cellar in my most disturbed of states.

Wendy and Justin Loasby who have just been there all along, always paying a visit. I have stayed in their home on a couple of occasions. Their daughter, Lou, who in the past couple of years came into my life – herself quite fragile and desperate to improve and break from the dreaded hold of depression. I am hoping she will write the preface of this book. Hold on, Lou!

I thank Karen Crussel who appeared on the scene when I most needed someone like her, a woman with faith and a true fighting spirit.

I thank also Patrice, who almost daily was by my side giving me encouragement and courage, himself deprived of work through back injury, and his lovely daughter, Celine.

I want to thank the whole team in the Centre Hospitalier in Luxembourg, for their magnificent effort, management, efficiency and professionalism. Unlike Ettlebruck, they respected me as a man. I was known as Mr Vaudrey. Mike, Johann, Fatima, Estelle and Sophia to name just a few who worked on this ward.

Marta, for constantly encouraging and supporting me following our break-up. It was for her after my first hospitalisation that I wanted to get back on my feet. To this day, Marta is still there on the end of the phone, busy with her own affairs, but serving me and my numerous needs. Cheers Marta. You are the best!

Fred Thomas for providing me with so much work on his incredible garden after my year out in Moscow. His aura forced me to do a good job, weeding his flower patches and more. I had some splendid moments in his garden. Thank you, Fred!

I would also like to thank his wife Marise, for her support and being there when I was most suicidal. Instinctively she knew when to ring. She is an amazing mother and I admire her for this.

The chaplain, Chris Lyon, persistently visiting after my car accident, being there in intensive care and pinning a cross on the bare wall.

My friends in the Orangerie, who give me a sense of duty and mission, visiting them and taking them out is always a pleasure. May you guys live for ever.

I mustn't forget Chantalle, a nurse in the CHL to whom I don't really know what to say. This last time in hospital we played ping-pong nearly every day. I thank her for her effort in giving me '*un gout de vie*' (a taste of life).

Big thanks to the Nelemans family, my godmother (aunt), her husband and my four cousins for putting me up last summer, for the conversations we had, and the food and badminton in the garden. To them, stay cool and pretty. We shall see each other soon.

I am enormously grateful to my new mates Dave Gibson and David Allcock. May the sun shine abundantly in your lives.

Ozlem and her boy, Keoma! 'We'll see us!' to coin the German.

To Lee Ray, my best mate at Durham, for putting up with a blubbery, sloppy guy. Shame about Istanbul. If you are reading this, then contact me, please.

And lastly, I thank myself for the effort I have made. I am very pleased and love myself more and more. Long live me! Hallelujah!

www.ingramcontent.com/pod-product-compliance
Lightning Source LLC
Chambersburg PA
CBHW031153250726

48655CB00002B/958